Thinking about the Seasons

Spring

Clare Collinson

SEA-TO-SEA
Mankato Collingwood London

This edition first published in 2011 by
Sea-to-Sea Publications
Distributed by Black Rabbit Books
P.O. Box 3263, Mankato, Minnesota 56002

Copyright © Sea-to-Sea Publications 2011

Printed in China, Dongguan

Library of Congress Cataloging-in-Publication Data

Collinson, Clare.
  Spring / Clare Collinson.
      p. cm. -- (Thinking about the seasons)
  Includes index.
  ISBN 978-1-59771-260-6 (library bound)
1. Spring--Juvenile literature. I. Title.
  QB637.5.C65 2011
  508.2--dc22

                                2009052820

9 8 7 6 5 4 3 2

Published by arrangement with the Watts Publishing Group Ltd, London.

Planning and production by Discovery Books Limited
Managing editor: Laura Durman
Editor: Clare Collinson
Picture researcher: Rachel Tisdale
Designer: Ian Winton

Photographs: Chris Fairclough: p. 17, p. 30; Getty Images: p. 4 (Ariel Skelley), p. 8 (Steve Satushek), p. 9 (Hermann Ayerbe), p. 10 (Image Source), p. 12 (John Giustina), p. 14 (Elan Fleisher), p. 15, p. 25 (The Bridgeman Art Library, p. 18 (Fiona Frank), p. 20 (Photolibrary), p. 23 (Peter Cade), p. 24 (altrendo images), p. 26 (David Tipling), p. 31 (David Rosenberg); Istockphoto.com: title page and p. 11 (Nina Shannon), p. 5 (Paul Tessier), p. 6 (Alexey Avdeev), p. 7, p. 11 (Nina Shannon), p. 16 (Andrew Howe), p. 21 (elena moiseeva), p. 22 (Tomasz Szymanski), p. 28 (Edyta Linek); Shutterstock Images: p. 19 (Losevsky Pavel), p. 27 (Bruce MacQueen), p. 29 (Olga Solovei).

Cover photos: Getty Images: main (Dev Carr); istockphoto.com: top (zts).

Page 9 *Landscape with a Rainbow* (1991), Hermann Ayerbe
Page 15 *Printemps à Giverny* (1903), Claude Monet
Page 18 *Path Through the Bluebells* (20th century), Fiona Frank
Page 25 *Duck and Ducklings* (c. 1890), English School

March 2010
RD/6000006414/002

Contents

When I think of spring, I think of bright sunshine and fresh air. The cold of winter has gone and I can play outside without a coat!

What makes you think of spring?

Spring is one of the four seasons of the year—spring, summer, fall, and winter. In spring, the sun gets stronger and the days get longer.

What kinds of flowers make you think of spring?

Spring is warmer than winter but colder than summer. In spring, the sun may feel warm, but the wind can be cold.

On windy days, I like to fly my kite.

What do you like doing in windy weather?

The March Wind

I come to work as well as play;
I'll tell you what I do;
I whistle all the live-long day,
"Woo-oo-oo-oo! Woo-oo!"

I toss the branches up and down
And shake them to and fro,
I whirl the leaves in flocks of brown,
And send them high and low.

I strew the twigs upon the ground,
The frozen earth I sweep;
I blow the children
round and round
And wake the flowers
from sleep.

Springtime makes me think of sunshine and showers. Strong winds in spring blow rain clouds quickly across the sky.

There is a saying "April showers bring May flowers." What do you think this means?

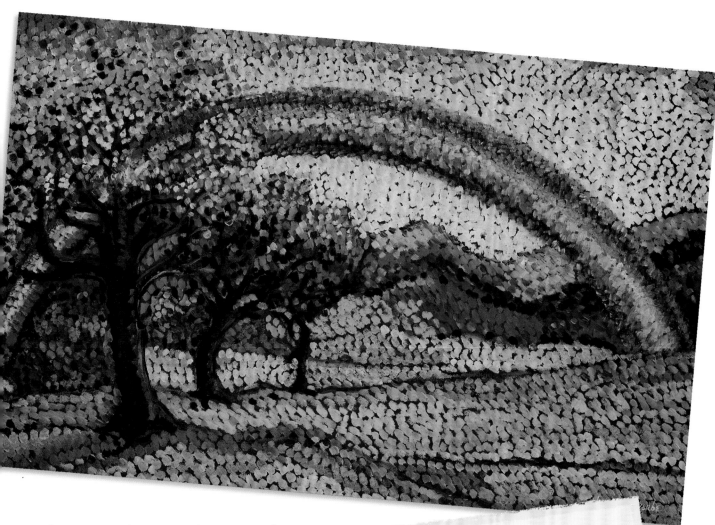

Sometimes in spring it is rainy and sunny at the same time. Then you may see a rainbow in the sky.

Can you see all seven colors of the rainbow in this painting?

When the air is cold in spring, I wear clothes that will keep me warm. I wear pants and a sweater or jacket.

The weather can change quickly in spring, so it's a good idea to wear lots of layers.

On sunny spring days, I can play outside in a T-shirt. After the cold of winter, it's nice to feel the warm sunshine on my skin.

What clothes do you wear in spring?

I like to go for walks in spring. When I
go outside in showery weather, I wear
a raincoat and boots in case it rains.

The Rain

Pitter-patter raindrops,

Falling from the sky.

Here is my umbrella

To keep me safe and dry.

When the rain is over

And the sun begins to glow,

Little flowers start to bud

And grow and grow and grow.

Have you seen trees covered in bright green leaves in spring? Some trees lose their leaves in the fall. In spring, when the weather gets warmer, buds open and new leaves appear.

In springtime, I often see fruit trees covered in pretty blossoms. This painting makes me think of apple trees in spring.

Where do you see blossoms in the spring?

I look forward to hearing the sounds of spring. The sun rises early and so do the birds. I sometimes hear them singing at dawn, as soon as it gets light.

In spring, playgrounds are full of the sound of children having fun. After the cold winter months have passed, I like to spend more time outside.

What other sounds have you noticed in spring?

This painting makes me think of the woods in spring. The leaves on the trees are young and small, and sunlight shines through to the ground.

Have you ever seen "carpets" of wildflowers in spring?

I like to go to the woods in spring. The air feels fresh and you can smell the sweet scent of spring in the air.

Do you like going for walks in the woods?

In springtime, I like to plant lettuce in the garden. Spring is a good time of year for planting. The soil becomes warmer and plants grow quickly.

As they grow, I make sure the young plants do not become too dry. Plants need water to live and grow.

What else do young plants need?

When I go to the countryside in spring, I often see tractors in fields. Spring is a busy time for farmers. They prepare the soil and plant seeds.

Have you ever visited a farm in spring?

How do you think a scarecrow helps to keep birds away?

Farmers sometimes use scarecrows to protect their crops from birds. They dress them in old clothes and sometimes fill them with straw.

Springtime makes me think of new life. Lots of animals are born at this time of year. On farms, sheep give birth to lambs and cows have calves.

This painting makes me think of new life in ponds and rivers. In spring, you can sometimes see ducklings learning to swim.

What kind of food do you think ducks like to eat?

Has a bird ever built a nest near to your home?

I sometimes see birds collecting twigs and straw. Spring is when birds build nests and lay their eggs.

Among the trees
Is a bird's nest,
And in the nest
Her three eggs rest.

And in each egg—
Hush, you'll be heard!
There lies asleep
A tiny bird.

H. N. Bialik

If you see a bird's nest, why should you not touch the eggs?

Springtime makes me think of spring celebrations. At Easter, I like to paint eggs and make Easter decorations.

Have you ever been on an Easter egg hunt?

On Mother's Day, I make my mom a card and give her spring flowers.

Can you think of any other special days in spring?

As the spring goes by, the days get longer and warmer. After the short days of winter, it's light enough again to walk through the park after school.

What do you like doing after school in spring?

In late spring, hot days are not far away. I get out my shorts ready for the fun days of summer!

Index